Wonders

Poetry from the heart

Wonders
Poetry from the heart

Mohan Balgobind

STERLING PUBLISHERS PRIVATE LIMITED

STERLING PUBLISHERS PRIVATE LIMITED
A-59 Okhla Industrial Area, Phase-II, New Delhi-110020.
Tel: 26387070, 26386209; Fax: 91-11-26383788
E-mail: ghai@nde.vsnl.net.in
www.sterlingpublishers.com

Wonders
Poetry from the heart
© 2004, Mohan Balgobind
ISBN 81 207 2758 4

PRINTED IN INDIA

Published by Sterling Publishers Pvt. Ltd., New Delhi-110 020.
Laserset at Vikas Compographics, New Delhi-110020.

Mr. Balgobind,

Thank you for sharing your poetry with me and for allowing me into your thoughts and feelings.

Your poetry is graceful and honest ... and saturated with metaphoric colour. Your talent lies in your ability to not merely transport your reader to your moment, emotion or thought, but in guiding him to truly engage in it ... (in my humble opinion!)

I hope others will one day have the pleasure of sharing your gifted craft.

Adriana Dibiase

Contents

Part I — To my wife

Part II — To my sons

PART I
To my wife

The many verses I wrote
speak of my love for you

A hummingbird

I asked
a hummingbird
to send Love my way.
It said to me,
"Love needs
to be thought;
Love needs
to be jolted;
It can never be bought."

As it buzz'd
floating back and forth
it sang:
"There is no puzzle
about Love's act.
It knows no prayer,
it's a fact.
It just knows how
to illuminate
the heart
and how to sparkle
the eyes.

"Love just knows
and in that knowledge
creates perfection
to the light
of the soul.

"Love sees no one
yet everyone.
It does not say 'please'
but comes to you
like a breeze."

O hummingbird

Tell me, O hummingbird,
    Tell me what is love
Which dwells within the heart
    And sent by Cupid from above.

O lovely bird who sings all day,
    What are its joys? What are its woes?
What is it to love a woman
    With cheeks like cherries, lips like rose?

My heart is dark without true love,
    It feels like a dreary night.
O sweet bird, have pity on me,
    Lead me to love's soothing light.

Sing to me the silky glory
    Of its arrows made of roses!
Oh, tell me of a female beauty
    With wondrous strides and high reposes.

Show me a woman to love,
    A woman who loves me too,
Whose fragrance is a new born rose,
    Who dances and sings like you.

Searching for my true lover

Over the ocean
I've been searching
Searching for my
True dear lover.
When I find her
I will give her
My heart, my soul
To discover.

Far I travelled
Empty hearted
Searching for my
True dear love.
When I saw you
By your window
My heart did leap
From that arrow.

Up in New York
Down in Georgetown
Searching for my
True dear lover,
When I saw you
Smiling at me
I knew of love
Instantly.

At the feet of your fence

(i)

Do you remember that day
    When you were peeping from your window?
The rain had just passed and gone
    And the brilliant sun cast'd my shadow.

Do you recall that same day
    I went at the feet of your fence
And your mother showed me the way!
    I saw you watching with innocence.

I do remember seeing you
    With your hair like silky clouds
And your pretty dress of white and blue.
    Honey, you're the prettiest in the crowd!

I wanted to reach out my hands
    And touch your tender cheeks,
I wanted to converse with you
    Until the night began to peek.

But little did I realize then
    That on me your head you'll rest,
Little have I thought of then
    That one day I'll feel your hair on my breast.

Dearest love of my life,
   Those memories are now old
But I always dream and remember
   The many promises I've told.

Many years have passed, retired
   Yet I've not achieved my goal
But the light in me has not expired
   And many old promises I still hold.

(ii)

It was
   your unique shyness
which first suggested to me
   that I
was attracted to you.
   It brought to me
a strange desire
   of fulfillment
of longing.

So many years have passed
   yet
I still remember
   the time
place
   circumstances
but

above all
    I still remember
how the earth melted
    under my feet
and how I was left sailing
    like a feather
in space
    at the feet of your fence.

I *recall*

I recall
my excitement
flew high
like a balloon
sailing in the sky
as we walked
hand in hand
for the first time
going to a matinee.

I recall
how
that evening gazed on us
so jealously
so happily
so admirably
and how
the cool evening sun
washed your pretty cheeks
how the soft wind
played with your hair.

I recall
the purple dress you wore.
It made your beauty
stick like glue
in my soul.

And nothing was the same again

(i)

We returned from the movies
and you and I together
for the first time
were left alone.

You were standing there.
(Darling, you never told me
what was running through your mind
that moment
when the earth stood still.)
I stretched forth my arms
and gently held your tiny shoulders.

The moon was full,
we were under the shadow of your house
so I could not see your blushes
I could not see your starry eyes
looking back at me
from behind your glasses
but I felt that little girl in you
frightened
full of innocence
full of questions.

Then
my youth spoke to me:
"You must share your first kiss."

18

My hands moved slowly
and I held your soft cherry cheeks
and like a butterfly to a rose
I felt my lips drawn to yours
and they touched gently
in total ecstasy.
And nothing was the same again.

(ii)

That night
my true love
you quivered my soul
with your honey so sweet
your essence so pure;
you brought to me
your bright reflection
your peace
your true affection.

The rain

(i)

Last night
the rain came.
It said to me,
"The joy of your life
has come."

Out of the dark clouds
the voice came
and spoke so gently
as the leaves danced
with the wind
and the clouds sailed
with its rain.

I was happy.
Softly I stepped outside
and felt the breeze
and the rain
on my face
and I felt
the wet grass
on my feet.

The night
consumed all of me
in its darkness.

The rain
drenched down my hair
and soaked my soul
with its warm
whispers and kisses.

Suddenly
it was over.
The sky was clear
the stars laughed again
in their black velvet bed
of space.

Then
I felt my hands
holding yours
and I was warm all over
with your love.

(ii)

O my love
my heart was filled
my heart was filled with love
my sweetheart's touch was warm.
It filled my life with ecstasy
morning
noon
and night.

Three tiny stones

An aristocrat
East Indian
a Guyanese
in Water Street
Georgetown
dedicated to gold
gold jewellery
eyed us with jealousy
yet like a businessman
he showed us
earrings
matching necklace
bracelets
and a diamond ring.

My bride-to-be
nervous
shy
looked at the ring
with disappointment
yet acceptance.

I spent all
of my meagre savings
for my wedding.
Oh, how I wish
I could've
bought her a better ring!

But though inexpensive
the three tiny stones
represented
myself
herself
and our love
in the centre.

Fly away with me

Yes, my love,
come
fly away with me
to Canada
just the two of us.

There
we shall sing like two birds
in the morning breeze,
and when you ask of our tomorrows
I will kneel down at your feet
and you will look into my eyes
and you will see
laughter
love and life
and all the happiness that awaits you.

Yes, my dear,
together
you and I
will pray, will sing, will watch TV
and you will tell me stories of old
and I will tell you stories of love.
Then I will sing lullabies
to put you to sleep
in a land
far far
away.

(ii)

I
was a king
to my people,
I came from Canada
to marry
the queen of your people,
and during my stay
with you
I felt piercing eyes
everywhere
and each time
I saw
how you blushed
and got prettier.

Like two dandelions
soaring high in the sky
clinging together
drifting in the wind
floating in love
      in pride
      in joy
we had no misgivings
and
we'd stolen the love
of our people
just for a little while.

The morning after

Everyone saw us then,
knew
we were the newlyweds.

We were up early
we watched the morning wake
we listened to the quiet sunrise.

I tied the bow
on your long black hair
I felt your young shyness
and loved you all over again.

Passersby waved at us.
They recognized us
we recognized them
they were our neighbours
our friends
our family.

A couple of sparrows
played among the hibiscus
the soft morning breeze
played with the leaves.

Please! Please!
Do not pull the curtain
on this moment
I do not want this to end
Let it be
a never-ending beginning.

It was our honeymoon

I've awoken before my wife.
I knew
she was very tired from our journey
so I must allow her to sleep.
Her back was turned towards me,
I looked around
and noticed many reminders
of my first visit here, in this room
in central Manhattan.

The sorry square still squeezed
and the musky smell
took me instantly
to my stay in this room
not too long ago.
The foul air seeped through my nose
travelled into my veins
my bones.
'Twas the stench of old manure.

She always wanted to see this city
and she was happy to be here
so I completely suppressed my dislike
and summoned excitement
for her sake.

Quietly
I rolled out of bed
walked to the window
and once more
I was completely amazed
at what was staring back at me
from across the street.

She turned over
with a deep restful sigh.
It then occurred to me
that the memories I'd gather
this time around
would be joyous
exciting
lasting.
After all
it was our honeymoon.

In that slumber
I knew she was somewhere else.
I watched my girl in bed
sleeping like a child
I saw what I saw in her face
for the first time
and I thanked God for giving her to me
and allowing me to bring her
to the Big Apple
where we would begin our lives
together.

I leaned back on the ledge
with folded arms
and gazed at my newly-wed wife
for the longest time
and a feeling of contentment
a feeling of joy
a feeling of excitement
drowned my entire being.
Only newly-weds
deeply in love
would feel
what I felt that day.

Finally
her eyes were opened.
My young wife looked at me
she blushed in her innocence
so alluringly
I could not resist.

I always remember

I always remember
the pretty doll who was entirely you
in your burgundy dress
and long black hair
that fell like clouds.

The you
even in a thousand years
will remain fresh
because it was not someone else.

That day
I married you
I wanted to say
Why me?

When I was looking at you
that moment froze.
I still see you new
as I will forever
a pretty you.

I wanted to hear you talk more
as we walked home
and the sun was trying to sleep
but there were jealous eyes
all around
and I did not hear enough.

That night
I sat to write you a letter
in which I wanted to say
how much I love you
but it seemed as though
the doll in you
had soaked up all my words.

I still remember
the way you looked back at me
when I took you home
lovely
innocent
untouched.
Oh, how I wish I relived
that evening!

There was nothing of us
before
and everything of us
after.

We became us.
The you in you
took me out of the then me
and blotted out my loneliness
and created the now me.

Go not, pretty one

Go not, pretty one
    From my throne so high
Go not, lovely one
    Till this first night passes by.

Rest on my silky throne
    Like a violet in the night
Rest your head on my chest
    Honey, it is so right.

I see in your cheeks
    Roses in the garden
I see in your eyes
    Starlight in the heaven.

I see in your lips
    the smiling petals sweet
Spread your dark hair
    On my silky, golden sheet.

Music in the south
    Is never so sweet
Like words from your mouth
    Each time we greet.

Roses in the hedge
    Their beauty will fade
But beauty like yours
    Is richer than jade.

Fairest of the fairs

O you
fairest of the fairs
come
sit by me
be my love tonight.
What will be must be.

O you
fairest of the fairs
come
I will take you
over the hills and the valleys.
We'll play in the dew.

O you
fairest of the fairs
come
take my hands
fly with me to the moon.
Now you know my stand.

I'll be there for you

Yesterday the dawn came to us
    And it is here today.
Tomorrow it will rise with no fuss
    Watching while we pray.

So, fear not, my sweetest love,
    My love for you is true
And like the sun guiding a dove
    I'll be there for you.

Where there's love there's truth
    (Of which I am so blessed).
Without you I have no strength,
    Life would have been so stressed.

Believe me, my sweet darling,
    My power will be poor
If you are not beside me smiling
    And open up my next door.

Like the sun I'll be there
    To light your every way
I will love you and I will care
    And protect you every day.

My wife

You are my life
    You are my dream
You are all I am living for
    You are my queen
But, oh,
    You are my wife.

Can joy be found
    In another ground?
Through His grace
    We found a common place.
The sun, the moon
    The stars —
They are all mine
    They smile to me
Even at noon.

And when the world
    Is not so fair
And life is not so clear
    My wife, my pair,
Will smile
    And then
Thing'll be clear.

The world of love
  Dwells in your heart.
How like a pretty dove
  You are blessed from above!
Your charm
  To me will never depart.
Our hearts are one
  Our souls communicate
We are so intimate
  We sing one song
Which He did create.

All mine

Oh, how you use your smile
That souvenir smile
I so love to see!
I love to hear you talk
and feed on the rhythm
of your rose-like lips —
they please me still.

You were the first one
who opened up my love
like the coming of a rose
at the breaking of the dawn.

You were my first love
You caused me to sing.
I sing the image of you
dwelling deep in me.

The many songs I sing
speak of your love in me
and my honesty.
To you
the many verses I write
reflect the emotion
in me for you.

But
are you not my precious pearl?
Are you not the gem
that brightened my heart
to reveal my strong love?

The perfection in you
made you mine.
You were mine yesterday
You are mine with today's passion
you will be mine with tomorrow's years
just mine
all the time
all mine.

Reading

You wear
that strong look
of intelligence
with your glasses
suited for a judge
but oh,
you are my sweetheart
reading a book.

We will still laugh and play

Because I could not stop for you
    You lovingly stopped for me;
You gave me your hand, your heart,
    You gave me love and tranquility.

At first we happily walked and played
    But those delightful years seemed like days.
We had no hurry, we had no care,
    It was fun, frolic and fair all the way.

We surpassed our relatives and friends,
    We showed them an example or two.
We walked along a bed of roses.
    Honey, it was all because of you.

We passed a life where our boys grew,
    We were ordinary dad and mom.
We passed the field where prosperity grew;
    So plenty was the honey and the blossom.

And now it seems like only yesterday
    Heart to heart we headed this way.
Though tomorrow bears no certainty,
    I am sure we will still laugh and play.

Every race we must run

The day will come
When we will say,
Bring back to us
Those golden days.

I'll love you still
Come what may.
You make me happy
Each night and day.

Guide us, O Lord,
Through night and day.
We do our duty,
To you we pray.

When it's all said and done
We will have our fun.
Until then, my love,
Every race we must run.

I love looking back

I love
looking back
to see the then me
standing between you
and my two boys
in summer
in winter
while I played the music
from our homeland.

I love
looking back
to feel the inside in me
changing
knowing that the me
within
was growing
maturing
because of your presence
    your love
    your commitment
to your household.

I love
looking back
to feel the steady presence
of a forward moving life
that changed our every tomorrow —
which was never clear
but
challenging
uncertain
rewarding.

Cheer is our true moral

Wake up, sweet darling!
The morning is here
Soft snow is falling
Christmas is in the air.
The sun has long risen —
It's hidden in the white.
Awake, my love, my pigeon,
I'll hold you with might.

Come, see the lamp post!
It's so white with snow!
Let me cradle your beauty.
Christmas cheers will glow.
I hear the sweet strain
Of children singing carols.
Though we are true Hindus
Cheer is our true moral.

Continue to be

Continue to be
the person you are
continue to live
your life the same

for if every person
were such as you are
and every life
were the life like yours

then this world
would be for sure
just the splendid way
God meant it to be.

My beautiful lady

My wife
my beautiful lady
walking in the evening
on Kimber Crescent
saying
"Hello, neighbour"
to every passerby.

Every evening
she walks out of her porch
with humility in her eyes
and youthful grace in her strides.
"Come,"
she says
"Come walk with me,"
and together
we will drink the nectar of the dusk
together
we will watch the sun falls asleep.

You and I

Darling
thirty years ago
it was just you and I.
Then someone said something —
our marriage
will never fly —
oh, how you cried!

But
you and I
never once said goodbye.
Everyone who sees us now
soaring so high
flying in the sky
they have raised brows
for you and I.

Yes
some fine morning
when the sun shall bathe our wrinkled faces
some boy and girl in love
will look at us
and smile
and wish
to be
you and I.

Second spring

They call it second spring
for you and I, dear one,
heart to heart we've come
through thirty-two years on a journey
where there is no second chance.

We stood on the hills of Antigua
counting the sailboats going by,
we rode in the guiding-tour car
in St. Kitts, watching
the tall grass played in the hot wind.

In our honeymoon we climbed
the Empire State Building
yet it was not as high as our souls
and, honey, there was no pretence
of our joy sharing it together.

Yes, my love,
the fire still burns in my heart
and at sixty the ice has not yet gnawed
at my attraction for you
but when the fire in us cools
and the iceberg erodes our fertility
will we think of each other
the way we do now?
Will we have the moments
to romance the way our hearts say?

In our lives there is this aimlessness
of a road that leads to blurred turns
but within there are sparks
which lead us somehow
to that somewhere
that something
for survival
comfort and peace.

Please realize, my love,
That our style
        our passion
        our lives
glow jealously deep in vindictive eyes.
Now our golden age draws near
and thirty-two years of travelling
in winding blurred pathways
are beginning to show
golds and diamonds
to brighten our way.

When body and mind
no longer have the strength
to see the stars at night
and appreciate the smiles
we now share,
when we cannot say
the moon is full,

will we forget our struggles?
will we forget our past?
will we see each other but not notice?

That won't happen to us
we may say
yet life is such.
If we could be someone to each other
in our final days
then our journey will not be in vain.
We are strong and fresh still
because dark shadows did not follow us.
Let it be the same
till we become memories.

On our anniversary

After
so many years together
you are still a stranger to me
you capture my love
you capture my heart
each time I see you in my way.

Every day
you bring to me
a whole new reason for living
for another day
in this world
in your arms
with your love.

Oh
how strange it is
I cannot say
because you look so fresh to me each day.
If this is love
then let me be
still innocent
by you
I pray.

It is so much you

It is so much you
who has given me
thirty-two years of me
and I have given you
through those years
thirty-two pounds of more you.

You and I have created
rooms in our hearts
big enough to hold
all of you and all of me.

The day we got married
so many years ago
I saw the full moon
sitting on your shoulders:
a light with no blemish.

Now
look at your reflection.
You will see what years and I
have done to you
but, dearest love,
the goddess of beauty
may no longer care
'cause our years and bodies
are moving in opposite ways.

Yet
when the children of man
look at you
your eyes
your face
your you
they see pride
they see beauty
dwelling in the now you.
They see a woman
they can only hope to be.

You brought to me
a you that was fearless
a you that was fearful
a you that grew to be
lovelier to me each day.

If the god of purity
examines you
even he will be jealous
of his creation.
Your innocence of youth
turned to matured wisdom,
a thing untouched by most.

To you I owe

To you I owe
the glitter of my delight
that began the day
I saw you peeping
from the corner of your window.

To you I owe
the glimmer of my hope
the quickness of my thoughts
which you awaken every day.

To you I owe
the rhythm of my mind
that governs my morning pen
which brings forth our strong unity.

To you I owe
the comfort of my days
the slumber of my nights
the steady heartbeat of our years.

When I am old

When I am old
and lay in bed
and my death pillow
is under my head,

just before
my world end'd
'cause my tired heart
no doc could mend,

when all my tears
have dried away
and my feeble lips
have nothing more to say,

even then, my love
I never want to see
my enemies
beside me bent.

I do not want
to see impostors
to see hypocrites
disturb my last few breaths.

Sweetest love of all

Sweetest love of all,
    If Death should come my way,
'Twill be not because I called
    Or I had a weary day.
If He should pass and knock,
    'Twill not be 'cause we failed
To land on solid rock
    And leave behind a happy tale.
If Death should say, "I am here.
    Your stay is now over."
'Twill not be 'cause you didn't care
    And the world we failed to discover.

O you treasure of my soul,
    We have flown the skies
And achieved our desired goals
    And all our dreams realized.
You have taken me to a place
    Far beyond the reach
Of many who ran the same race
    Heading for the glorious beach.
Yes, you have revealed to me
    The limitless reaches
Of the horizon and the seas
    And their heavenly beaches.

So when it comes that I
　　My last breath must sigh
And it's time that I must die,
　　Honey, you must never cry.
My journey was for you,
　　O you wind of my life,
'Cause everything I do
　　Is meant only for you, my wife.
So when I am no more
　　For you to rest your head,
Just think that I'm with a friend
　　And will be soon in bed.

My final breath

When my final breath I take
    Let not any teardrop shed
Let no sadness darken the space
    When to heaven my soul is led.

In my final space of silence
    Let silence merge with quietude
Let every eye and head bend low
    And pray for my state of solitude.

Let the vastness in the airy sky
    Echo with the sound of singing
And let the drums and the brassy bells
    Take away every step of mourning.

Let the pundits preach from the holy books
    And let my family clasp their hand
And pray for my soul a permanent place
    With the gods and the angles in graceland.

I've lived a life of joy and peace
    But now my journey's ended.
Oh, how I cried when I came to be!
    So let my soul in Krishna's realm be blended.

I leave behind my many years of past
    I leave behind the seeds I did sow
But above all I leave behind
    A world of sadness, pain and woe.

So let me be the dead I am
    And let me fly away in peace
And let me see all happy faces,
    Then with joy this life I'll release.

O hummingbird

O hummingbird
I want to thank you
And count my blessings,
I want to count them
One by one to you.

I came to you
When sadness evaporated
All my hope for joy,
And you brought to me
The magic of Love
That you perceived
As a divine plan.

In that magic of Love
You created for me a plan
And you took me by my hand,
And the world of wonder and beauty
Unfolded within my mind.

The magic power of Love
Created in me a song.
I took your spell and found
That the rhythm of that song
Enraptured my errant mind.

Now, O hummingbird,
The wonders of the world are open'd
And the stars above are singing:
They are singing about my glory,
And, O bird, I feel like a king.

In the magic of these moments
Eternality springs to me
A light of hope
A plan of peace
A life with Love
In a divine release.

PART II

To my sons

I taught you to fight with words
to know when to run
to be free like the wind
but unlike the wind
to know when to stop.

Counsels to my sons

My sons, there will be days
when you will want to sit
and ask counsel of your past.
I hope I'll be beside you
long after my mortal breath
and you will see in me
through my eyes and words
the eternal richness of our people.

There were no promises made
by my father, nor his father,
that life will consist of oneness
and our thoughts will be unbounded
and our hopes will be divine.
But promises were made
that someday somewhere
our hearts will meet again
and melt into one omniscience —
but only if our Vasnas allow it.

In the midst of a culture
with variety and with zest
with silence and with despair
with certainties and with unknowns
you have to make a place
for yourself and for yours.

Those who prepared their life paths
know where to stop
and rest their heads in comfort.
Those with worn-out soles
know where to find replacements.

But you cannot find comfort
in another's path, another's shoes;
not even your Vasnas allows this.
Only your karmas will take you
in the road you prepared.

You come from a rich race.
Your people are shy and silent.
We have always accepted strange ways
with gentility and respect
like a stream flowing silently
that cannot avoid the rocks thrown.
Yet the rocks which were thrown
never prevent the stream
from reaching its destiny
with an unfoldment of bliss
where the waters meet and merge.

Like the stream
you too must follow your road.
But how must you avoid
the solid rocks protruding,
to maintain your steady course
of certainty where our hearts will meet?

Look back at those days
when the rain fell...
the wind in its might
pushed the heavy clouds
from its path of infinity
and the sky became blue again.
Look back at those days
when the dense fog was lifted
and the grass twinkled like diamonds
and the sunshine brightened the dawn.

Your hearts now beat
in a rhythm of gladness
because your karmas let it happen.
Now each dawn of sunshine
brings forth a day of magic
with whispers of hope and joy.
Listen to those whispers
and you will realize
what makes the moon glow
and what makes the stars twinkle.
What fills your heart with delight
is what makes your night into day
and fills your weakness with strength.

But when it's time
that you have come to know
that there is something else
for your being a human,

that there is a deep hidden reason
for your soles to leave their prints
upon this earth,
   would your awareness rapture your desire
and open like a morning lily?

What will your answer be
to the ones who'll take your name
when they ask of the stream you left behind?

You must realize your complacency
and be aware of your actions
for you cannot control destiny
and you cannot erase your karma
but you can control identity
with your divine mortality.

Our teachings are wise, my sons,
and our ways are good
but only to our people.

If you like the flame
that is now burning in you,
learn of its effects
so you can withstand its heat
and bear its burning for life.

When you enter into a strange newness,
bewilderment creeps in late
like an ugly spirit which will not depart.
It will torment your soul

and our hearts will never merge
if you allow it to remain.

I have taught you
our heritage, our truth.
Use them for observation
and then lay down your rites.
Only then the ugly spirit will vanish.

Do not let greed replace goodness.
Yet see yourself as a mortal
and recognize what you can changes
and what you cannot
and let your omni-action take hold,
for you will have to contend
with that which you cannot change.

When I am no longer around
for you to read my ways,
you will see beyond the present
a vision of me and our people
and we will watch your actions.
We will be there
at the end of the stream
where our hearts will meet —
but will they merge?

Fear

Every father keeps trying
to explain to his children
how horrifying it was
when he was coping with a fear;
how terrified they all were
of something they could not explain
of something they could not control
because everything went round and round
and their fears kept coming again and again
in the continuous wheel of birth and death.

In our beginning
we come into this world in fear.
We do not know what is that fear
but we echo'd the world
with our first cries
knowing — perhaps —
that the beginning to an end is now.

As human beings
after a million years
of trying to explain our fears
the closest we ever got
is that it involves resentment
which in itself cannot be explained
except to say that this life
is not where we prefer to be.

In the middle
between our beginning and our end
we realize where we came from
and where we are heading.
This realization generates the fear
which fathers try to explain.

Lost

Every one of us
sometime in our lives
on this long and unpredictable road
we travel
find ourselves totally lost.
You forget where you came from,
and the many exciting plans you made
yesterday
are lost in an obscured whiteness
floating in the morning dew
that hug the grass.

You feel
as if
you have left a landmark somewhere
and now you are looking for it.
Again and again
in circles
you search
for that landmark in that whiteness
but can't even find a trace.
You bump yourself
on stones
on trees
yet
that landmark seems lost forever.

Angry
confused
blinded by that whiteness
only determination and hope
keep you searching
because deep within the boundaries
of your brain
the landmark exists.
You know it's real.

Then
one day
just by accident
it's there
smiling at you
in a brightness you never saw before.

Goodnight, Dad

Many times
I asked myself
"What's real?"

Every day
the dawn arrives
and the evening
rolls away
faithfully
in the horizon
all around
and I say
"This is real."

But when
in my home
my little son
is missing from
the dinner table
and his voice
is not there
to say
"Good food, Mom!"
my mind
searches around
the empty rooms
telling me

"This is not real
this is not happening
to me."

I feel sad
every day
not for loss
not for love
but for a smile
and a voice
that says
"Goodnight, Dad."

Ways

Your youthful years are here;
    Gather their ways with pride
Cause all the unknown things you do
    On the path you pass they ride.

Follow your dreams with dignity;
    This flower of yours is short.
Your lines are drawn, your karma's set;
    Never put the horse behind the cart.

Like the map of our Toronto
    Your course is destined for you.
Only when your ripe age comes
    Will the ways you gather serve you.

Tornadoes

Our lives are filled with tornadoes
    as our years grow in numbers
We gather diamonds and stones
    we maintain our best to avoid their plunders.

We bask in the sun one moment
    and forcefully fetched away the next
We stagger, we fall, yet we fight —
    to fail has no pretext.

When your tornadoes strike
    your fate will be determined
When their forces passed and gone
    you will stand tall and cemented

For you have looked into their eyes
    and braved their vicious velocities
You've never let their angry funnels
    pull you into their gravities.

You sift the diamonds from the stones
    and you live to relate the tales
With pride, courage and dignity
    your offspring will fight their hails.

You asked me

You asked me
Dad
does the road
always wind uphill?
and I said
Yes, my son
so long as
there is desire
      ambition
      satisfaction
in you,
your road will wind steep.

You asked me
Dad
what will I find
at the end?
and I said
My son
you will find
a resting ground,
you will climb no more.

You asked me
Dad
will there be peace?
and I said
That depends
on the seeds you sow
on the road
as you go.

My two sons

You my two sons
are merited guys.
With my limited means
I taught you my best.

I send you on to errands
hidden and vague
with objectives attainable
in a four-fold divided world:
    ambition
    greed
    jealousy
    hate —
the roots of all evils.
Day in, day out
they rule the east and west
north and south.

I've lived more years
seen more places
achieved my goals and dreams
all with pride
    honour
    joy
    love
still

I fear the tomorrow's world
for its four-folded ways
    its uncertainty
    its instability.
But you must face them
and reach for your sack of gold
as I did.

I point you the way
knowing darn well
the challenges
the struggles
the hardships
that await your everyday path,
the fights
the groans
the sweats
you must bear
from those of unethical ways.
But
the satisfaction derived
the happiness gained
will depend on your final treasures.

God appointed me your provider
    your teacher
    your protector.
I taught you to fight with words
to know when to run
to be free like the wind,
but unlike the wind
to know when to stop.

My sons
you are governed
by minds of your own.
You are fruitful-spirited men
you do not feed on imitations
and you loath dejection.

So
I ask of you two
to create an alliance
combine your best fashions
your best boiling brains
and shoot out like one arrow
to places others only dream of.

The road of knowledge

Let me drink from your fountain
    where wise men assemble
Let me smell the smell of ink
    and let me be where students think
Let the urge to learn flow freely
    for years to come through my veins
And let my blood stained with greed —
    cause wanting to read is my creed.
Like a raging wind inside of me
    The road of knowledge I must seek.

Karma I

Karma is reality.
Though
it will not say
what it knows
yet
it will do
what it must.
It does not fly
from me to you.
You cannot erase karma.

At *age sixteen*

So at age sixteen
I watched myself falling
    falling
    falling
like someone sliding
down the side of a mountain.

They said I was a man
riding on empty slopes.
Myself said to me
you are a youth
full of desires and hopes
you are not pretending.

Look down
I said to me
The valley is not far.
It may seem
bathed in sunshine
with flowers, birds and bees
glowing enchantingly.

Believe not what you see
from a distance
they said.

Tomorrow's confidence
is today's planning.

At age twenty

Here
like a rooster in the rain
I wait
in my room,
window covers in silky thorns
piercing my inner self
like giant spikes.

Now
hope fading fast,
days pass like years
sky grows greyer.

Unwillingly trapped
squeezing tighter
in a square
trembling
terrified
sleepless
secluded
sore

at age twenty
I see no silver lining.

Time

Time slips away
unrecovered.
Look fast.
It moves, tick-tock,
unreturnable.

I sat on my years

And
I sat on my years
watching my future
grow bleak,
withered petals
strangling
in the vines of reality.

Dusty yesteryears
dark memories
drifting down winding lanes
like beetles crawling
in the bones of the dead.

The warm sunbeams
stabbed like swifts.
Unfinished dreams
crammed my space
with grey-webbed woes.

The truth must hurt —
sometimes.

I felt myself falling
falling into the claws of regrets.
And
I sat on my years.

Still

Happy
yet
dissatisfied
un-peaceful
inside
outside.

Give me more time
I pray.

Or
take me back
to a new starting-point.

You see
it doesn't happen
suddenly
unknowingly.

Oh yes
it took years —
years of hope
expectations
disappointments.

Now
at sixty
life's empty...

Still.

Karma II

Follow your karma as you go
    Strengthen your wisdom in your youth
Leave no stone unturned as you flow
    What's hidden there may be the truth.

Like the skeleton of a leaf
    Your karma is written in your palms.
Many of your plans may wither away
    But do not detour from your aims.

You'll never know the worth of the seeds
    You sow and the fruits they'll bring.
Only age will truly perceive
    How your karma flows and swings.

Dear Father

Dear Father
like a hungry babe
waiting to pull on soft nipples
I long to be with you.

I crave for your arms of comfort
like the sea
washing upwards
reaching for your calm.
I lift my head
on a pyramid
and call out your name
and echo the heavens
and the stars
that fill your eternal nothingness
with your supreme diamonds.
I walk on the sandy shores
and listen to the white shells
and I remember you.
I remember my years of youth
and I see my days of tomorrow
in their dead whispers
of lamentation.

Deep in the heart of the dead fields
I hear
the dry wind moan dirges of me

as the dead stock stands still
in its unweaving browns
that hang like my tomorrows.

Dear Father,
ocean of mercy,
I wait for you
wrapped in this eternal deathlike maze
waiting for this stream in me
to lay still and cold
and rot in an unmarked hole.

This squeezing square space

I always remember
the view from my window
the first time I woke up
in the city that never sleeps.
From the third-floor view
Thirty-fourth Street was asleep;
'Twas a valley in the Rockies
where cars evenly spaced
like beetles
on the seat of steep stone.

I always remember
how amazed I was
at the skill of modern man.
Now their skill
was staring back at me
from across that valley,
and the how-who-built-what feelings —
the feelings I initialized
for New York City
from radios, books and school —
came alive like heating cold porridge.

It was middle Sunday morning
facing the severest snow storm in years,
Manhattan was completely covered
with a blanket of silky white flakes.

There were no birds chirping in the trees
to cheer and comfort my weary ways
There was no smell of roses in the air
to welcome another newborn day.

With the mucky smell of sealed space
the piercing sound of soundlessness
I was the only man on Earth
in a tiny box closing in on me.

But hark! There! A pair of pigeons
loving on the window sill.
They woke me from my seclusion
to welcome this wintry chill.

Oh, how I envied them!
Not because they were pretty.
The Big Apple belonged to them;
'Twas their hope, their home, their destiny.

I passed through this populous city
many times in my learning journey
And each time I imprinted in me
my hope, my home, my destiny.

Of all the cities I learned about
their architecture
their customs
their traditions
I remembered only one,
but now this city has detained me
just for a little while
'cause a tangled feeling in me
was telling me to free my self
from that squeezing square space.

The streets of Harlem

An old man
sat on his front porch
in an old bamboo chair
a dirty cloth-bag at his feet
and on his lap
the Holy Bible
dilapidated
ancient as the reader himself.
His black unshaven face
baked in the hot afternoon sun
and his glasses
sat unused
before his closed eyes.

Beside the porch
there was a ladder
leaning on the wall.
There was a pail
and some dried-up old rags
under the window
of several broken panes.
Everywhere
the houses seemed abandoned
rusty wires hung everywhere
singing of better times,
and broken sheds
spoke of neglect and sadness.

There by the side-door
a heap of broken plaster
and chopped timbers
mixed with yesterdays' prints
and other litters
created infestations,
and the polluted yard
in a mixture of
nature and filth
gave rise to unwantedness

Reading of New York
I pictured perfection
I imagined spectacles
of beauty
of wealth
of glitter.
Now
walking in the streets of Harlem
my dreams felt betrayed
and died
in an anarchy
of deprivation
of wretchedness
of poverty and shame.

Every street cried
of dilapidation
of abandonment
of dumpiness,
and the air reeked
of oldness
of filth
of death.

Here and there
patches of trees
gave a hint
of the prosperity
of yesteryears
but today's sunrise
brings sorrow, pain, neglect.

Is that our destiny?

Lord
I am like a poor farmer
who destroyed the face of nature
and burnt the only bridge of hope.

Tell me, O Lord
Should I leave New York City?
Should I return home
empty-handed
sullen
lean
dejected?

I feel myself all raked up inside
with harrows of barren clay
where even the best fertilizer
in the whole wide world
does not encourage growth.

There is still the you in me,
for I long to sit on my porch
sipping lemonade
bathing in the hot wind
soaking in the tropical music.

'Tis your presence in me
that allows me to feel
that going back home I'll be

a dry tall tree growing on rocks,
a dirty dull dog chewing on steel chain,
seeing withered meadows of nothingness.

Yes
I see you in me, Father,
rusting in the hole
I crawled out of not so long ago
and famishing in a den
of disgrace
   dejection
   drudgery.

Lord
tell me
Is that our destiny?

St. Kitts

Broad
sunny blue
sandy shores
palm-leaf sheds

Lofty hills
undulating golf course
singing palm trees
scatter sugarcane fields.

Wind
hot
white
dazzling
rolling.

Waves
howling
roaring
splashing
washing.

Black
shining
glowing
smiling
friendly.

Bridge
old
humped
cracking
dying
weeping.

Brook
Indian blood
stones mourning
trees bowing
water clear
    stained red
    singing dirges
    in St. Kitts.

Grandkids

A man's greatest wish
is to sit in his front door
watching his grandkids
playing in the grass
in the quiet dusk.

A man's deepest joy
is to sit by his fireplace
watching his grandkids
playing on the floor
with their talking toys.

A man's satisfaction
is to sit at the dinner table
watching his grandkids
stuffing their messy mouths
with thick red ketchup.

Grandparents

The gossips of our grandparents
muffled from toothless gums
as they coughed and yawned with contentment.

The smell of backyard tobacco
chimnied through their aged nostrils
dissipated in the breezy spaciousness.

Men and women ceremoniously stuffed
their rusty -"chillams" and joked about
their age, their success and their failures.

Nothing was hushed, unmentionable
age was pride, children were joys
and wrinkles signified labour and pride.

Old men massaging unshaven chins
in their long, silky Indian suits
which bathed in the aroma of tobacco.

Covered in their own perfume of "pan"
the old women spat blood-coloured spits
from their rusty-coloured stained lips

as they rubbed their ancient legs
plaited their long grey and black hair
desperately trying to impress the circle

of their lineage and their achievements
their children, their grandchildren and great-grands,
the most significant assessment of one's wealth.

They came from the old countries
young, ambitious and bonded.
Now freedom filled their air and eyes.

As they counted their friends dying
they too realized that they were waiting
waiting on time with pride and accomplishment

making themselves ready for a silent heart
pleased that now they were never ignored
and their voices listened and heard

their anger and their needs respected
their laughter and their advice longed for
in the evenings of songs and flickering flames.

They were the individuals of our past
they asked for little. Their needs were little
and their days were copied over and over

because they had long since given up
the desire of fashion and beauty
but embraced the things of value.

Some died by sickness, some by age
Some in their sleep in the quiet dark
but all in peace — for they were never forgotten

they were never left in a world
of loneliness, in squeezing squares
but were always around: the aged and the young.